Your Baby Is Safe

an illustrated book

for anybody who has loved and lost a little one

For Isadora & Trey ~M.Y.I.

Published by

In association with The Midnight Orange

and

Text copyright Melissa Yuan-Innes © 2011

Artistry & photographs copyright D. Antonia Truesdale © 2011

Cover layout by Stephanie Mooney © 2011. All rights reserved.

Author photograph © Jessica Sarrazin, 2010

All rights reserved. No part of this book may be used or reproduced in any manner whatsoever without written permission except in the case of brief quotations embodied in critical articles and reviews.

For more information, please address Olo Books at http://olobooks.wordpress.com/
or D. Antonia Truesdale http://themidnightorange.com/

Your baby is safe.

Your baby loves you.

You did not do anything wrong.

Your baby may be singing
with other babies in heaven.

Your baby may be reborn
into another life.

Your baby may be resting.

Take care of yourself.

Take the time to mourn
in your own way.

Work will always be there.

If you push too hard
or too soon,

you may hurt yourself even more.

You are a mother.

You are a father.

You loved your baby.

You cared for your baby as best you could.

That's what parenthood is.

Your faith may be shaken—

In yourself,

In your partner,

In your God.

Your baby still loves you.

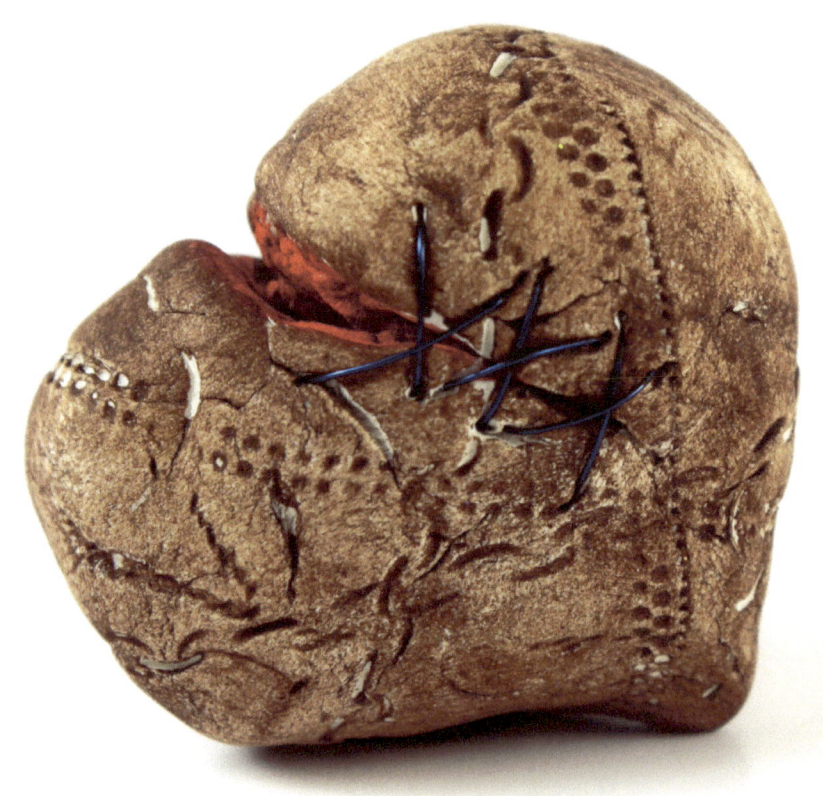

You may be angry.

You may be surprised
at how much people care about you
and are sorry for your loss.

You may be surprised

how indifferent people seem.

People will say hurtful things.

Forgive them.

Eventually.

Your baby loves you.

You don't win any prizes
by keeping a stiff upper lip.

You can't force yourself
or your loved one
to "move on."

Give it time.

Mom, your body is different now.
You just had a baby.

Try to be gentle with your body
even though it didn't sustain this tiny life.

Rituals can help you heal.

Have a ceremony.

Write a letter to your baby.

Light a candle.

Plant a tree.

Your baby loves you.

Horrific things happen.

You are still a good person.

You will get through this.

Your baby loves you.

You need tenderness.

If the people around you can't give it to you,

find someone who can.

If nowhere else, somebody's always awake on the Internet.

"A broken heart is an open heart."—Rumi

Maybe you can reach out to someone else.

We are all broken people.

Sometimes.

There is still hope.

You will know if and when you're ready to love another baby.

If you're trying to have another little one, good luck.

Inform yourself.

But also make sure you find joy
in things that have nothing to do with babies.

Some day, when it's time,
you and your baby will be together.

Your baby is safe.

Your baby loves you.

Your baby forgives you.

Forgive yourself.

www.ingramcontent.com/pod-product-compliance
Lightning Source LLC
Chambersburg PA
CBHW042004150426
43194CB00002B/116